Vladimir Putin's Holy Mother Russia

A Biography of the Most Powerful Man in Russia

Anna Revell

Copyright © 2017.

All rights reserved. No part of this publication may be reproduced, distributed, or transmitted in any form or by any means, including photocopying, recording, or other electronic or mechanical methods, without the prior written permission of the publisher, except in the case of brief quotations embodied in critical reviews and certain other noncommercial uses permitted by copyright law.

This book is intended for informational and entertainment purposes only. The publisher limits all liability arising from this work to the fullest extent of the law.

Table of Contents

Tensions in Ukraine

Rise to power

Civil War

Holy Mother Russia

Putin, the Tsar and the Church

Putin the Man

Putin and Syria

Putin's Other Hotspots

Putin and Trump

The Third World War

Tensions in Ukraine

If a war between the western nations breaks out again it could very well start in the east. The First World War began with the assassination of the heir to the Austro-Hungarian Empire in the town of Sarajevo, in modern day Bosnia- Herzegovina.

The Second World War started with the German invasion of Poland in 1939.

The state of Ukraine, also in Eastern Europe, is also a cause of tension. In this case the relations of the United States and their European Allies on the one side, and the Russian Federation and its allies on the other, have been sorely tested by events in that country.

Ukraine occupies the vast steppes between European Russia and the Black Sea. The country has several important rivers. The most important river is the Dnieper, which flows into the Black Sea and divides the country. Its capital is Kiev.

Ukraine has a long and checquered history. With few natural defenses Ukraine came under the influence of its powerful neighbors. At various times the land was ruled by Lithuanian, Poland, the Mongol Empire, the Ottoman Empire and lastly by the Soviet Union.

When the Soviet Union collapsed and splintered in 1991 Ukraine declared its independence.

At first the economy of the new nation suffered from inflation, poor economic growth and widespread corruption.

By 2004 however things were beginning to look up, though there were still serious problems that needed to be addressed. There were human rights abuses, the concentration of power in the hands of the President, and, persistently, government corruption.

Then Viktor Yanukovych, serving as Prime Minister, was elected President in 2004 under suspicious circumstances. The Supreme Court ruled that he had rigged the election in his own favor.

A peaceful public protest that has been called the Orange Revolution overthrew

Yanukovych and installed Viktor Yushchenko as President.

The nations of Europe were intensely interested in the Ukrainian situation. The European Union and the United States wishes to see a democratic, pro-European regime in Kiev.

The Russian Federation, the successor state to the Soviet Union, was anxious that it should not have a neighbor which would join the European Union and became a member of NATO.

NATO is an alliance of 28 states including the United States. It was founded to contain the Union of Soviet Socialist Republics.

With the Union dissolved it seemed its purpose needed to be redefined.

Ostensibly that purpose is to 'maintain the security of the North Atlantic area'. However the Russian Federation believes its aim remains the containment of Russian influence.

Europe and the United States attempted to influence the election of 2004. Pro-Yushchenko activists received funding from a number of foreign donors including the US State Department.

When Yanukovych was returned all 25 members of the European Union withdrew their ambassadors from Kiev. The United

States likewise refused to recognize the result.

The Russian Government gave help to the Yanukovych campaign which including advice on vote rigging techniques.

The President of the Russian Federation at the time was Vladimir Putin. Indeed, he still is.

Vladimir Vladimirovich Putin was born in Leningrad (now called St Petersburg) on October 7 1952. He was the youngest of the three children of Vladimir Spiridonovich Putin and Maria Ivanovna Shelomova.

His brothers Viktor and Albert are both dead. Albert died in his infancy while Viktor fell to diphtheria during the horrific Siege of Leningrad during World War II.

Putin's father served in the Soviet Navy. His mother was a factory worker.

Putin studied law in Leningrad in 1970 and was required to join the Communist Party.

When he finished his degree in 1975

He decided not to pursue a career in law. Instead he joined the KGB.

'You know, I even wanted it,' he said.' I thought I would be able to use my skills to the best of society.'

The KGB or Committee for State Security was established in 1954 and was one of the most effective and influence intelligence-gathering agencies that has ever existed.

So powerful was the KGB that when Mikhail Gorbachev introduced sweeping reforms to the Soviet Union, including curtailment of the powers of the KGB, its Chairman Vladimir Kryuchkov attempted to overthrow him.

The coup failed and the KGB was divided into 5 separate agencies.

A man such as Putin with intimate experience of espionage methods might be expected to find rigging an election or raising support for his own presidential candidate fairly easy.

But why was the President of Russia so concerned that a pro-European such as Yushchenko should not lead Ukraine?

To understand this we need to appreciate something of Russian geography and history.

Russia is a vast country. It is the largest nation in the world, covering 6.6 million square miles. It borders 14 countries.

Its size has made defending Russia a serious problem, and especially in the west where there are few natural boundaries.

By natural boundaries we mean mountain ranges or rivers that could be used as natural defenses.

Russia has been invaded several times. The Mongols conquered Russia in the 13th century. The French almost succeeded in the early nineteenth century, as the Germans did in the 1940s. So the fear of encirclement and invasion is perhaps understandable.

When the Soviet Union split into 14 separate republics in 1991 the problem for Russia was compounded. It was now surrounded by states it had formerly controlled.

These states were now open to influence from the United States and the European Union, an influence these powers were happy to exert. Russia feels it is in danger of being surrounded by a bloc of pro-western, potentially hostile countries.

That it is why Putin believed he had to ensure that Viktor Yanukovych, who favored close associations with Russia, became President of the Ukraine.

It should be conceded that Russian concerns have some foundation.

The European Union has declared closer economic and diplomatic ties with former Soviet member states such as Ukraine, Armenia, Belarus, Georgia and Azerbaijan to be 'a key element in EU foreign relations.'

Three former Soviet states, strategically located on the Baltic: Latvia, Estonia and Lithuania are already members of the European Union and NATO.

The United States in recent years has pursued a policy of limiting Russia's influence by strengthening the European Union and Russia's neighbors and in particular by interventions in Ukraine.

There is the perception in the US State Department that growing Russian nationalism needs to be contained.

Unsurprisingly Russian foreign policy perceives the United States in the same light.

The security of the Black Sea ports in Ukraine was also a concern for Russia. Before the dissolution of the Soviet Union, Russia had unchallenged access to the Black Sea trade.

That trade might be threatened by a hostile Ukraine.

The Russian Federation also maintains a fleet in a number of Black Sea ports.

But in any event the people of Ukraine had spoken. A bloodless revolution had forced a re-election which brought in Viktor Yushchenko.

But who had elected him? The re-run election of December 26 had given Yushchenko just 52 per cent of the vote.

The vote was roughly divided along geographical lines. The west and the south-west, including the Crimean Peninsula, generally supported Yakunovych.

The electoral boundaries roughly corresponded to ethnic boundaries.

Those who had elected Yushchenko generally spoke Ukrainian, while those for Yakunovych were generally Russians or Russian –speakers.

The country was divided along ethnic lines and by a close election. There was the potential for civil war.

Yakunovych remained a powerful leader, a focus of anti-European opposition, and in 2009 he ran again for the presidency.

He was elected with only 49 per cent of the vote. He was inaugurated on February 25 2010.

President Yakunovych stalled negotiations to join the NATO alliance (initiated by Yushchenko), declaring that Ukrainians didn't want to join.

He was open to cordial relations with Moscow and expressed support for Russia on issues such as natural gas supply, the status of the Russian Black Sea Fleet and the refusal to recognize the independence of the Republic of Kosovo from Serbia.

He did however continue to endorse Yushchenko's policy of integration with Europe and promoted a degree of co-operation with the NATO alliance.

This infuriated Moscow. At this time Putin was no longer President. The Russian Constitution forbade the president from serving more than two subsequent terms.

However Putin was still in charge. The very day after the new president, Dmitry Medveded, took office he was appointed Prime Minister.

Prime Minister Putin declared to President George W. Bush that 'Ukraine is not even a state!' He later referred to the country as 'little Russia.' During a NATO summit in 2008 he had threatened to annex eastern Ukraine and Crimea.

In 2007 he had also accused the United States, perhaps with some justification in the light of the 2003 Iraq War, of exercising 'almost uncontained hyper use of force in international relations.'

Putin seemed to be posturing for a showdown with the west.

Yakunovych was playing a dangerous game, trying to hold a strong position between Europe and Russia.

Meanwhile he was consolidating his power at home. In October 2010 the Constitutional Court greatly expanded his powers.

In 2011 the opposition leader Yulia Tymoshenko was arrested on charges of abuse of power during her term as prime minister. She was tried and imprisoned.

Timoshenko's former Interior Minister was sentenced for four years on similar charges.

In 2012 the President's own Party of Regions won the majority in the parliamentary elections. Yakunovych's Party of Regions nominee, Mykola Azarov, was returned as Prime Minister.

Both the European Union and the United States criticized the election, citing alleged voter fraud and vote-rigging. US Secretary of State Hilary Clinton said that the election represented a 'step backward for Ukrainian democracy.'

There were however conflicting reports on the fairness of the elections. The European Academy for Elections Observation stated that they were 'in compliance with democratic norms', though they had been married by irregularities.

Whatever the truth of the matter, the reaction of western politicians and media was feeding the already deeply discontented opposition in Ukraine.

It seemed the Azarov Government would go ahead with plans to integrate with the European Union.

However, on November 21 2013 the government refused to sign an Association Agreement with the European Parliament.

Azarov cited 'the national security of Ukraine' as justification. Instead he proposed a compromise: a three way agreement between the European Union, Ukraine and Russia.

At this time Putin was again President of Russia. His press secretary and spokesperson, Dmitry Peskov, declared the decision to be 'an internal and sovereign decision' of Ukraine, adding however that the Federation would consider Azarov's proposal.

Europe however accused Russia of exerting pressure on Ukraine.

Yakunovych and Azarov prevaricated. They kept the prospect of signing an agreement with Europe open, and the Union was eager to keep the offer on the table.

At home the Ukrainian government was facing intense pressure. Thousands of protesters took to the streets, demanding that Ukraine join the European Union.

By December 8 there were almost 8 million protesters in Independence Square, Kiev.

The government passed laws to repress the protestors. Clashes followed.

In February 2014 Yakunovych offered to form a new government with opposition leaders, but it was too late. A compromise could not be reached.

On February 22 the Ukrainian Parliament removed Yakunovych, who had already fled to Russia.

Olekdandr Turchynov, Speaker of the Ukrainian Parliament, was chosen to be President.

His successor, Petro Poreshenko now presided over a deeply divided country. The ousting of Yakunovich alienated hundreds of thousands of Ukrainian citizens in the east.

From his refuge in Moscow the deposed president called upon Putin to intervene. The United States and the European Union stood behind their man Poreshenko.

The battle lines were drawn and Putin was ready to make his move.

Rise to power

It will be useful to pause here to consider Vladimir Putin and how he came to power.

When the KGB was dissolved he turned his back on Communism. With the fall of the Soviet Union it was clearly a spent force and offered no prospects for advancement within the new Russia.

In 1999 he described Communism as 'a blind alley, far away from the mainstream of civilization.' He refused to participate in the failed Soviet coup of August 1991.

He cultivated the friendship of Anatoly Sobchak, the Mayor of his home city,

Leningrad, but now reverted to its former name, St Petersburg.

Sobchak (d. 2000) was one of the authors of the new Russian Constitution and was regarded as a mentor by Putin.

In May 1990 Sobchak appointed Putin as an advisor on international affairs. One of his responsibilities was the promotion of foreign investment.

Within a year of his appointment Putin was investigated for understating prices of goods for export.

He survived the affair however and in 1994 was appointed Deputy Chairman of the St Petersburg government.

In 1995 he organized the St Petersburg branch of the Our Home is Russia Party, an organization supported by many of Russia's right-wing elite including President Boris Yeltsin and Prime Minister Viktor Chernomydin.

Sobchak was not re-elected Mayor of St Petersburg in 1996 and Putin was appointed Deputy Chief to the Presidential Property Manager in Moscow.

This was an influential position. The Manager, at that time Pavel Borodin, a man who was arrested in 2001 in New York for money-laundering, is responsible for the administration of federal properties.

In March 1997 the then President Boris Yeltsin made Putin Deputy Chief of the Presidential Staff. This gave him intimate knowledge of the President and his circle, and access to the President himself.

In 1998 Putin was appointed Director of the Federal Security Service, the primary successor of the KGB. Having trained as a spy he was now the head spy. But his meteoric rise has not ended.

The Prime Minister of Russia in 1999 was Sergei Stephasin. Stephashin had also previously served as head of intelligence.

He had been appointed the year previously by Yeltsin. The Constitution of the Russian

Federation gives the President wide-ranging powers.

He appoints the Prime Minister (or more properly, the Chairman of the Government of the Russian Federation), ministers and other state officials with the consent of the Duma (Parliament).

The President may initiate legislative bills, suspend the laws in some circumstances, dismiss the Prime Minister and order new elections.

The President also has extensive powers in the field of both foreign affairs and domestic policy.

In Russia the Prime Minister exercises a largely administrative role. The President is not required to appoint an elected member of the Duma.

Yeltsin was a powerful man and used that power. He was the last President of the Soviet Union and the first President of the Russian Federation. He had thus overseen the transition from Communism to federal democracy.

Indeed, he had been instrumental in the fall of the Communist Party and the opening of Russia to liberalism and the free market.

He saw himself as the stabilizing guide Russia needed during this turbulent time.

In choosing a prime minister he was not looking for someone with whom he could share power. Rather, he was looking for a successor.

The Constitution of the Federation allowed the President only two consecutive terms. His second term was to end in 1999.

Yeltsin was looking for a strong hand who would continue to govern Russia in the manner that he had done.

Sergei Stephashin was not that hand, despite being a Yeltsin loyalist. The President did not consider him a viable successor. The previous Prime Minister, Primakov, had been dismissed for that reason.

On August 9 1999 Yeltsin made Putin one of the three Deputy Prime Ministers. Later that same day Stephashin was sacked and Putin appointed in his place, on the condition that he would run for the presidency.

Still on the same day Yeltsin publicly endorsed Putin as his successor. He was so confident of his choice that he saw no need for a respectful distance between the prime ministership and the presidency.

So Vladimir Putin was about to become the highest officer in the land after only 9 years in public office and having never been subjected to public scrutiny.

Putin was relatively unknown at this time. His appointment came as a surprise to many, both in Russia and overseas.

The real rulers of Russia- rich oligarchs who dominated the State Duma- were happy to accept him however.

The transition from communism to capitalism was high-jacked by a number of ex-Soviet leaders and entrepreneurs who controlled most of the wealth and resources.

To facilitate the transition from state-owned property to privatization Yeltsin had distributed stock freely to Russian citizens using a voucher system.

Ostensibly it was a shrewd scheme. However, most of the shares were bought up for cash by a small number of individuals who intent on making themselves rich.

Indeed they become extremely rich while the great majority of Russians became extremely poor. The oligarchs came to dominate Russian politics. Yeltsin had now created a beast he could not control.

The oligarchs financed the re-election of Yeltsin in 1996. Yeltsin was now beholden to them.

Although the exact nature of Putin's appointment remains murky it is clear that Yeltsin chose a man who he believed would keep the status quo. Putin was a man the oligarchs could trust, though as they would discover, at a price.

Rumors also circulated that Yeltsin was about to be caught up in some financial scandals and he needed someone who would protect him.

The war against the rebellious Republic of Chechnya was going badly and Yeltsin's health was going the same way. He had a history of heart disease and underwent heart surgery in 1996.

These factors are alleged to have precipitated the president's surprise resignation on December 31 1999, at the end of the third year of his second term.

Putin was now Acting President. His first decree granted immunity to the former president from charges of corruption.

The presidential elections were held on March 26 2000. Putin stood against 11 candidates, the most prominent of them being Gennady Zyuganov, Leader of the Communist Party.

Despite being a virtual unknown Putin chose not to personally participate in public debate, nor to use the free television and radio time accorded all candidates.

Commentators attributed this decision to reluctance to discuss controversial and potentially damaging issues such as the campaign in Chechnya, his relationship with Yeltsin and the oligarchs.

During the campaign the state media was perceived as favoring Putin, while pressure was exerted on private media outlets to ignore or misreport rival candidates,

PACE (Parliamentary Assembly of the Council of Europe), an organ of the European Union that observes and reports on democratic processes, reported that the media in general was being pressured by government agencies.

It also documented instances of fraud in the elections.

Putin won the election with 53%. Immediately he set about consolidating his presidency. He began an attack on the oligarchs, promising to end their influence and the corruption of power.

The first great volley was the arrest of Vladimir Gusinsky, a Jewish media giant who had not supported Putin during the election.

During the election he also initiated a media investigation linking terrorist attacks attributed to Chechen rebels to the FSB, the state intelligence agency.

Gusinsky was charged on June 13 2000 with misappropriation of funds and imprisoned at Butyrka, an overcrowded prison built in Soviet times for political dissidents.

Other charges against prominent business leaders followed.

After two months Putin called for a ceasefire. On July 29 Putin met 21 of Russia's most powerful oligarchs.

He told them that their power over Russian affairs was over. Their man Yeltsin was gone and he was in charge now.

But that meeting was not so much a surrender of the oligarchy but an alliance. Putin agreed to cease the persecution. He would allow the oligarchs to retain their property and power in return for their support for him alone.

One of the oligarchs at the meeting was Vladimir Potanin. He was responsible for the share distribution scheme that created the oligarchy, and was its greatest beneficiary.

He described the meeting as one of partners rather than enemies. 'The oligarchs are tired of being enemies and want to be loyal citizens,' he said. He said that Putin would meet these 'loyal citizens' on a regular basis.

Putin was not taking a huge risk in confronting the oligarchs. He already had a new power base in Unity, a conservative and Populist Party created for the December 1999 State Duma elections.

Kremlin insiders helped to form Unity and both Yeltsin and Prime Minister Putin supported it, in return the party supported Putin in the presidential elections.

In December 2001 Unity merged with Fatherland – All Russia and Our Home - Russia to form United Russia, the largest political party in the Duma. In 2017 it held 76% of the seats and is pledged to support the policies of President Putin, without whom it would not have existed.

Putin was elected for a second term in 2004. The Constitution forbade serving more than two consecutive terms but said nothing about non-consecutive terms.

On May 7 2008 the First Deputy Prime Minister, Dmitry Medvedev, was elected President. The following day he appointed Putin Prime Minister.

On September 24 United Russia nominated Putin their man for the presidency in 2012. It was understood that Medvedev would become Prime Minister, acting essentially as Putin's puppet.

On March 4 2012 Putin was elected to a third term amid widespread allegations of fraud made by opposition parties and foreign observers.

There was intense anger about the manner in which the unholy trinity of United Russia, Putin and Medvedev had colluded. So dangerous was the popular feeling that the government feared civil resistance such as had been seen in Ukraine in 2004.

Perhaps in anticipation of popular protest, President Medvedev had in 2011 centralized the organization of the Russian Police under the Kremlin's control.

About 100 000 protested Putin's inauguration, the largest demonstration in Russia since the end of the Soviet Union. While he was taking the presidential oath riot police were clearing peaceful demonstrations and arresting protesters.

A now powerful and confident Putin observed Ukraine's President Pereshenko sign the economic agreement with the EU on

June 27 2014. He had the Duma behind him. He had the plutocrats behind him. He had the military behind him. The fate of Ukraine was in his hands.

Civil War

Petro Pereshenko had been elected President of Ukraine on March 13 2014. He promised to mend relations with Russia and reconcile a divided Ukraine.

Eastern Ukraine was generally pro-Russian and protested the ousting of Yakunovich. There was also unrest in the mostly Russian speaking Crimea and there was talk of secession.

Putin was ready. He had plans for the annexation of Crimea prepared as early as February. He also had a written request from Yakunovich, now residing in Russia, to intervene in Crimea to 'establish legitimacy, peace and order'.

Moreover Sergei Aksynov, head of the Crimean Government, had made a similar request of Putin on March 1.

The Crimean Peninsula juts out into the Black Sea and is of great strategic value. The power that controls the Crimea controls the Black Sea, and hence has access to the Mediterranean, the Balkans and the Middle East.

For this reason the peninsula has long been a battleground for many countries. The Romans, Byzantines, Turks, British, French, Germans, Venetians, Genoese and Russians have all fought for control of the Crimean ports.

Historically the Crimea was vital to Russia for trade with the West. Russia's ports on the Baltic froze during winter, restricting trade, whereas the Crimea was much milder.

In 1954 the Soviet Union transferred the government of Crimea to the Ukrainian Socialist Soviet Republic. During the time between the transfer and the fall of the Soviet Union the Russian population of Crimea increased to almost 2 million. The total population was 2,280 000 in 2014.

In January 1991 94% of the populace voted to separate from Ukraine and become an autonomous republic under the Soviet Union, as it had been before 1954.

On July 16 of that year Ukraine declared its independence, and the Autonomous Republic voted to join Ukraine by a small majority.

On May 6 1992 the parliament of Crimea again voted, this time for independence. The proposal succeeded 128 to 18, pending confirmation by a referendum.

Kiev strove to prevent that referendum. It headed off the poll by granting Crimea autonomous status.

The move greatly exacerbated the tensions between Russia and Ukraine and complicated negotiations over control of the Crimean ports, which Russia leased from the Ukraine.

On March 11 2014 the Crimean Parliament met and declared its intention to separate from Ukraine and seek union with the Russian Federation.

In response the Ukrainian Government announced the creation of a National Guard.

At the same time Russian armed forces conducted exercises near Ukraine's eastern borders.

Talks between the United States and Russia concluded on March 14 without finding any middle ground on the Crimean issue.

On March 15, the day before a Crimean referendum on independence, 50 000 people marched in Moscow against intervention.

According to official reports 95% of the Crimean population voted in favor of independence from Ukraine and union with the Russian Federation.

On the following the Crimean Parliament officially declared independence and formally requested Russia to receive Crimea. The Ukraine Government, now led by Poreshenko, refused to accept the legitimacy of the parliament's actions.

On March 18 Putin addressed the State Duma, announcing 'two new constituent entities within the Russian Federation: the Republic of Crimea and the city of Sevastopol.'

A Ukrainian and a Crimean soldier were both killed in a controverted incident in the Crimean city of Simferopol.

On March 19 Russian soldiers crossed the Crimean border and took control of Ukrainian military bases.

Ukraine responded by authorizing Ukrainian soldiers to fire in self-defense but did not invade Crimea.

The President of the United States, Barack Obama, condemned Russia and praised Ukraine's restraint. He announced the possibility of sending troops to the Baltic States to reassure them against Russian aggression. However he ruled out military intervention.

The European Union likewise condemned Russia's actions.

The United Nations General Assembly passed a resolution declaring the Crimean elections illegal on March 27.

In April tensions escalated. A Russian infantryman shot and killed a Ukrainian officer at about the same time as Putin was authorizing Russian armed forces to assist Crimean defense forces. He threatened the Ukrainian Government with 'consequences' when Ukrainian forces killed several Russian servicemen.

Further acts of violence followed. In August Ukrainian troops resisted a Russian incursion against Kherson, a city mainly populated by ethnic Ukrainians.

In the following month Russia began a persecution of the Crimean Tartar minority. The Tartars were of Turkish origin and dominated the Crimea during the rule of the Islamic Ottoman Empire from the fifteenth to the eighteenth century.

The Tartar National Assembly was closed down. Activists were apprehended. Some disappeared without trace.

Russia was not only active in Crimea. The Donbass region in eastern Ukraine, named after the Donets River, is Ukraine's easternmost province and borders Crimea.

Donbass is a heavily industrialized region important for its coal. It produces about 30% of Ukraine's coal exports. It is also an important manufacturing region.

About 58% of the Donbass population is ethnically Ukrainian, though about 75% speak Russian. After the German occupation during World War II, Donbass was largely repopulated by ethnic Russians.

Following the removal of Yakunovich in 2014 there were widespread pro-Russian and anti-European protests in Donbass, as there were in other parts of eastern Ukraine.

Riding the wave of these demonstrations, separatists formed the People's Militia.

On April 13 the Ukrainian Government gave the Militia an ultimatum to disband. But fighting had already broken out between Government and separatist forces.

On April 15 the Ukrainian Government launched a full-scale assault. Civil war began in earnest.

Separatist forces were lead mostly by the ethnic Russians. The People's Militia was reinforced by troops from Russia and other states of the former Soviet Union. The Russian Government has always claimed these are volunteers. However, equipment used by the Militia is undoubtedly supplied by the Russian military. It is estimated that from 9000 – 12000 regular troops from the Russian Federation are involved.

President Barack Obama provided funds and military assistance to the Ukraine military. However he remained adamant that no US military force would directly intervene.

Likewise the EU has committed to only material aid, fearful that the Ukraine situation has the potential to escalate into a major war between Russia and its allies and NATO.

As of February 2017 the People's Militia controls eastern Donbass, centered on the principal cities Donetsk, Luhansk and Horlivka. Almost eight thousands soldiers have perished. Over 2000 civilians were killed, and two and half million Ukrainians have become refugees.

There have been 11 ceasefire attempts.

The fighting continues to the day this book is written.

It is as yet unknown what Donald Trump's election as President of the United States in 2016 means for the Ukrainian conflict. Trump has expressed admiration for Vladimir Putin and a willingness to mend the relationship with Moscow.

But that is a subject for another chapter.

A treatment of Donbass could not conclude without mentioning the tragic affair of Malaysia Airlines Flight 17.

The plane was shot down on July 17 2014 near the Ukrainian/ Russian border and came down near Hrabove in the region of Donetsk, territory controlled by the People's Militia. It had been on a routine flight from Amsterdam, headed to Kuala Lumpur.

All the passengers (283) and crew (15) on board the Boeing perished.

Investigations were hampered by separatists, but after intense international pressure Dutch investigators were given access.

They concluded that the plane had been brought down by a surface to air missile operated by separatists but launched from a Russian launcher. This was confirmed by US and German intelligence.

Russia denied responsibility and continues to do so. At first it claimed the missile targeted a Ukrainian jet. Later it claimed that Ukraine forces shot down the plane.

There is much speculation about what happened. Possibly it was a terrible mistake or an accident caused by inexpert operators. It seems incredible that someone would deliberately target a civilian aircraft, drawing international attention.

No-one has yet been made accountable for the disaster.

Holy Mother Russia

Before we can attempt to understand Putin we must attempt to understand Russia, for his sense of mission revolves around Russia.

The history of the Russian state began with the Varangians, who were Vikings from Scandinavia.

The Varangians penetrated the lands of the Slavs through the rivers that flowed to the Baltic, Black and Caspian Seas. They established themselves over the Slavs.

According to tradition the first Varangian ruler of the Rus, as their subjects came to be called, was Rurik. He was elected ruler at Novgorod, in the north.

Rurik's successor Oleg extended Varangian southward to Kiev.

From Kiev the Rus ruled the largest state in Europe and was one of the most prosperous, having access to rich trade routes to the east and to Constantinople, capital of the Byzantine Empire.

It was through the Byzantine Empire that the Rus experienced Greek Orthodox Christianity.

Vladimir the Great, revered as a saint in Russia, accepted Greek Christianity and was baptized. Medieval chroniclers relate how Vladimir investigated the merits of Islam, Judaism and Roman Christianity. The last he is supposed to have rejected on account of its lack of beauty.

Vladimir accepted Christianity on behalf of his entire country, and ordered his nobles to be baptized.

Over the course of time the Kievan empire disintegrated into various principalities.

It came to a final end with the invasion of the Mongols from the east in 1237. The Rus became subject to foreigners. Their rulers became vassals of an alien power, though they retained some degree of autonomy.

The Mongol conquest separated them from the West, and from this time Russians began to distrust foreigners and became more inward looking.

During the course of the 14th and 15th centuries the city of Moscow started to become powerful and became increasingly assertive in its dealings with the Mongols.

Ivan III (r. 1462 – 1505) finally defeated the Mongols and called himself Grand Duke of All Russia.

In 1453 an event occurred that would profoundly mould Russia's sense of identity.

In that year Constantinople was conquered by the Ottoman Turks, a people who, like the Mongols, had come from the east.

Constantinople was the capital of the Byzantine Empire, and the Byzantine Empire was the last remnant of the Roman Empire. The first Christian Emperor, Constantine, had transferred his capital from Rome to the city on the Bosporus that bore his name (it is now called Istanbul).

In fact the citizens of the Byzantine Empire did not call themselves Greeks, which was indeed the language they spoke. Rather they called themselves Romanoi, Romans.

The Byzantine Empire was considered the hub of Orthodox Christianity. Roman and Greek Christianity had split in the eleventh century and in Constantinople Roman Christianity was seen as an abominable corruption of the true faith.

With the Byzantine Empire gone, Moscow took the mantle of empire upon itself. Greek Orthodox Christianity had succumbed to the Turks. The Roman Church was in error. The Russian Orthodox Church was now spiritual successor to Contantinople and the last bastion of Christian civilization.

If the Russian Church was now the true light of the world then the Grand Duke of Moscow was protector and defender of the that light.

His office was sacred and he had the blessing of God himself.

In 1547 the Grand Duke Ivan IV (The Terrible) assumed the title Tsar.

Tsar is a Russian rendering of the title Caesar. Ivan became the Emperor of the New Rome.

Rome had been the first seat of the Empire. Constantinople was the second. Now that Constantinople was gone, Moscow was the 'Third Rome.'

'Two Romes have fallen!' proclaimed the Russian monk Filofey in the sixteenth century. 'The Third stands. And there will be no fourth!'

Thus Russia acquired a unique sense of identity, inextricably tied to Orthodox Christianity.

Turbulent times returned for Russia in the seventeenth century. The 'Time of Troubles' was marked by civil war, famine and incursions from the west, especially from Poland, which aimed to conquer Russia and convert the people to Roman Catholicism.

Eventually the Poles were defeated, and the victory was celebrated in Russia with National Unity Day (the Communism abolished National Unity Day, but Putin restored it).

A grand assembly of the Russian people then chose Michael Romanov to be the new Tsar.

Michael's successors, including Peter the Great and Catherine the Great made Russia world power, greatly extending its power across Asia and into the west.

Even though Russia re-established a relationship with the West it never really became western.

Rather it steered a middle course between the east and west, both of which were regarded with unease. The two pillars of the Russian state were the Church and the Emperor.

Russia became 'holy mother'. It was Mother Russia that drove the French under Napoleon from Russia in 1812.

It was Mother Russia that fought against the enemies of Russia in the First World War (1914 – 1918).

Except in that conflict she failed to save the Church and Emperor.

In 1918 the Communist Revolution overthrew them both.

Even under Communism the divine image of the divine Tsar seemed to be transferred to the new autocratic leaders.

The cult of Lenin spread through Russia and especially after his death, taking on an almost religious quality.

The same aura shone about Stalin and even today many Russians regard Stalin not as the murderous tyrant the West sees, but as the father of his people.

In 1991 the rule of Communism came to an end. It had lasted 73 years.

As great as its impact had been on Russian society, it was too short, surely, to change the Russian soul. After all, 73 years is a blink of an eye compared to over a thousand years of Russian civilization.

Russian still regards their country as having a unique place in history. They still regard the west and the east with suspicion. Perhaps history has taught them to be so.

They still prefer to look to themselves as the Third Rome and guardian of civilization.

The Orthodox Church has returned to the place in society it enjoyed for centuries. But the other pillar of society – the Tsar – is absent.

Or is he? Perhaps this is the role Putin sees for himself. Maybe he thinks he has been destined for it. Whatever his personal feelings about having power, it does seem to he believes in Russia's destiny, and that he has a key role to play in it.

Putin, the Tsar and the Church

Now we will look at the role of the Church in Putin's Russia.

The Russian Orthodox Church has traditionally exercised enormous power over Russia and the lands of the former Soviet Union.

As we have seen, in the tenth century Vladimir the Great, ruler of the Rus accepted the Greek form Christianity from the Byzantine Empire based in Constantinople (now Istanbul).

When Constantinople fell to the Islamic Ottoman Turks in 1453 the Patriarch of

Moscow declared himself sole head of the Russian Church.

For close to five centuries thereafter the Church has embedded itself in every aspect of Russian society.

To be Russian was to be Orthodox. To be anything else was to be an alien to the soul of Russia.

It was the mainstay of the Russian monarchy, sanctifying the decrees of the autocratic Tsars and guaranteeing the divine sanction on their rule.

That all changed in 1917. Tsar Nicholas II and his regime came down and with it the Russian Orthodox Church.

The new Soviet Union led by Lenin and after him, Stalin, saw religion as an ideological obstacle to a socialist Utopia.

Orthodox clergy, along with the leaders of other religions, were imprisoned and tortured or 're-educated'. Church property was confiscated. Churches and monasteries were destroyed or converted to government use.

What remained of the Orthodox hierarchy was so infiltrated by the KGB that critics such as the dissident priest Gelb Yakunin described it as 'a subsidiary, a sister company of the KGB.'

Religion persisted however. In 1987, on the eve of the fall of the Soviet Union, up to 50%

of Russians still baptized their children, while 60% requested Christian burial.

After Communism, Orthodoxy flourished again. It has pretty much recovered the place it had in society. Officially it is not the state church. The Russian government officially guarantees freedom of religion, though ties between church and state are close.

Vladimir Putin's own relationship with the Russian Orthodox Church appears to be close.

Putin's father was an atheist but his mother was devoutly Orthodox. She attended church regularly despite the government persecution. She secretly baptized Putin and brought him to religious services.

It is probable too that Putin was acquainted with Christianity is his role as a KGB agent operating in the 70s and 80s.

Putin says that his own religious awakening began in 1993, while he was working in the St Petersburg administration. His wife Lyudmila Shkrebneva had been involved in a serious car accident.

He continues to wear the baptismal cross his mother gave him and it is something of an open secret in Russia that Bishop Tikhon Shevkunov is his personal confessor.

Shevkunov is a cleric of radically conservative views and is seen to accompany the president on international trips.

And President Putin seems to suggest that the relationship between Church and State should be stronger. Interviewed by Time in 2007 he stated 'it is not possible today to have morality separated from religious values.'

In 2012 Patriarch Kirill of Moscow publicly endorsed Putin's third term. The Church hierarchy has expressed support for Putin's actions in the Ukraine and his domestic agenda, which includes the repression of gay rights.

Putin has enacted laws requiring religious organizations to be registered with the state. Organizations that do not register are dissolved by the Ministry of Justice. Some experience difficulties in registration and those that have often found it difficult to purchase land or build places of worship.

These laws favor the Russian Orthodox Church, which experiences no problem in registrations and seeking permits. Catholic, Protestant, Islamic and Jewish organizations have reported what appears to be state-sanctioned discrimination.

On July 16 2016 Putin signed legislation, veiled as anti-terrorist measures, which restricted the right of religious organizations to proselytize. The Russian Orthodox Church was exempted from the provisions of that law.

Perhaps the key to Putin's relationship with the Russian Orthodox Church is to be found in the response he gave to Metropolitan Hilarion, the foreign relations chief of the Russian Orthodox Church, when in 2012 he requested Putin to make the protection of Orthodox Christianity worldwide a priority.

Putin replied 'you needn't have any doubt that that's the way it will be.'

Now the protection of Orthodox Christianity even outside Russia was previously viewed within the domain of the Tsar of Russia.

The Tsar assumed the protection of Orthodox Christians living under Ottoman rule.

So does the Russian Orthodox Church believe Putin is successor to the Tsars?

It has been suggested that one of the motives for Putin's intervention in Syria on the side of the Assad regime is the protection of Syrian Christians in a land that used to be within the Ottoman Empire.

In any case the Church is certainly beholden to Putin.

For his part, he should surely feel empowered that the Church has backed him in much the same manner as it backed the ancient Tsars.

Putting aside Putin's personal religious beliefs, whatever they may be, there appears to be a mutually beneficial relationship between Church and the still officially secular state.

Interestingly the pre-revolutionary imperial regime seems to be undergoing rehabilitation in Russia.

In 1998 the remains of the last Tsar of Russia, Nicholas II of the House of Romanov and his immediate family, brutally executed by agents of Lenin in 1918, were interred at St Peter and Paul Cathedral, St Petersburg.

Then President Boris Yeltsin was present at the service. Also present were the living Romanov descendants, including Nicholas Romanovich (d. 2014), then head of the House of Romanov and heir to Nicholas II.

On August 14 2000 the slain Romanovs were officially canonized by the Russian Orthodox Church, designated 'passion bearers' who humbly bore their sufferings for the love of God and the Church.

Monuments to the Romanovs throughout Russia are being restored, such as a 6 meter high bronze statue in Moscow of 'the Liberator', Alexander II, who freed the serfs in the nineteenth century.

Putin appears on good terms with the leading members of the Romanov family, leading to speculation that he plans to restore the monarchy.

Archpriest Vsvevold Chaplin, a prominent spokesman for the Russian Church expressed the wish in 2015 for Putin or a Romanov to become Tsar.

Vladimir Petrov, a close associate of Putin and member of the ruling United Russia Party, has also wished for the restoration of the monarchy.

Putin has not made his views on the restoration of the monarchy clear, but it would certainly fit in with his vision of a strong Russia reasserting its influence under a powerful authoritarian government supported by a powerful Church.

It is perhaps significant that two other recent Russian leaders who exercised great personal authority, Lenin and Stalin, were endowed with a sacred mystique, much as the Romanovs were.

A recent poll indicated that one third of the Russian population was in favor of the restoration of the monarchy in some form, whether that be absolute, constitutional, Romanov or non-Romanov.

Putin the Man

In September 2015 Vladimir Putin spent a weekend with former Italian Prime Minister Silvio Berlusconi. They visited Massandra winery on the coast of the annexed Crimean Peninsula.

The winery was founded in 1894 by Tsar Nicholas II to supply wine for his palace at nearby Livadiya.

Berlusconi asked if they might sample the wine. The pro- Russian director of the vineyard promptly uncorked a bottle of Jeres de la Frontera, 240 years old and valued at $90 000.

Ukrainian prosecutors immediately began preparing a claim for damages. The President of Russia and former prime minister were drinking Ukraine's heritage, though Putin would surely have claimed he was drinking Russia's.

The image of Putin, uncrowned Tsar of Russia, drinking the spoils of victory with a former head of government criticized for corruption, abuse of power and control of the media seemed particular apt for the Putin era.

It becomes more so when one notes that the bottle of wine in question was produced when the Empress Catherine the Great was expanding Russia's boundaries and asserting herself as a world player.

The west tends to view Putin as a de facto Tsar of Russia, warmonger intent on restoring Russia as a superpower.

While this may be half the truth many Russians view him in quite a different light.

In his homeland he is seen as the strong, stable hand Russia needed after the turbulent transition from Communism. He has brought in a degree of economic reform but is essentially conservative, a mindset that seems to have suited Russia historically.

To many he is a protector, a 'little father', the title given by the peasants to their Tsar in bygone years.

Yeltsin's words to Putin when handing over the mantle of power were 'take care of Russia.' Putin regards himself as a Russophile above all else.

Putin is not a charismatic man. He tends to be a beauracrat rather than a populist leader. And he does genuinely seem to be devoted to his vision of what Russia should be.

His devotion to Russia is perhaps demonstrated by his marriage to Lyudmila Ocheretnaya (nee Shkrebnev).

Putin and Lyudmila married in 1983 and divorced in 2013. Lyudmila is supposed to have commented that Putin was first married to Russia. There was no room for her in the relationship. During her time as First Lady of Russia she kept a low profile.

Putin and Lyudmila have two daughters: Mariya (b.1985) and Yekaterina (B.1986). They have been kept out of the public eye and little is known of them. However Mariya is believed to be working in medicine.

It is rumored that Putin is presently spending time with a female companion.

Putin suffers from the burden of isolation. He sees the fate of Russia in his hands alone.

From where does he draw his strength then?

We have seen Putin's relationship with the Russian Church. Commentators have observed that this relationship goes beyond the domain of personal conviction.

He sees the Church and State as having a mystical and indissoluble bond. Orthodox Christianity is the soul of Russia and the source of its strength.

One of Putin's philosophical heroes is Vladimir Solovyov. Writing in the nineteenth century, Solovyov held that Russia's destiny was to resist the influence of both Asia to the east and Europe to the west. He believed, as many Russians did, that Russia was the Third Rome, after Constantinople and Ancient Rome, and the true spiritual successor to Christian Rome.

The philosopher Ivan Ilyin is another of Putin's inspirations.

Disillusioned with the Communist Revolution in 1918, Ilyin fled Russia and lived in Western Europe.

He was however dispirited by the west, writing that the advocates of western culture were trying to break Russia into 'twigs' and 'rekindle them with the fading light of their civilization.'

Ilyin argued against the totalitarianization of the state as much against the total democratization of the state. He advocated a 'third way', a distinctly Russian way.

Here it is significant to note that although Putin's rule is certainly authoritarian he appears to be careful to preserve basic liberties, at least for Russian citizens.

Both Ilyin and Solovyov were monarchists.

The image of Putin that frequently comes to us through the western media is of a man of action – a bare-chested, hands-on macho man who seems ready to wrestle a bear.

Putin is genuinely fond of fishing, skiing, Judo, cycling and other sports. But it seems out of character for the private and secretive President to be seen publicly enjoying these activities.

He is enthusiastic about promoting a healthy lifestyle, though perhaps there are political reasons too. If Putin sees himself as the embodiment of the Russian state and people then he should be seen to be strong and athletic.

Putin is immensely wealthy, though his actual wealth cannot be estimated. In 2012 he reported his own income as $113 000. However his fortune is believed to be in the billions.

Putin and Syria

In 2003 the United States and its allies, the 'Coalition of the Willing' as the alliance was called at the time, invaded Iraq and deposed the dictator Saddam Hussein.

After a war that had been declared illegal by the United Nations the US replaced the government of Iraq with an American style democracy.

Thereafter western commentators, acting out of what must be described as arrogant optimism, predicted that a wave of revolution would overthrow other Arab regimes and replace them with liberal democratic regimes amenable to the United States and Europe.

What actually happened, as foreseen by political and military analysts, was a seismic fracture of the Middle East.

Iraq itself split into multiple ethnic, political and religious factions, the nominal government struggling to keep control.

The power vacuum created by Saddam's overthrow was filled by radical Islamic organizations, the most powerful being the Islamic State of Iraq and the Levant, otherwise known in the west as ISIS or ISIL.

As of March 2017, the tyrannous reign of ISIS extends across northern Iraq and western Syria and notoriously attacks many countries of the world by terror.

Nevertheless there were signs that the liberalization of the Arab regimes in the Middle East and northern Africa might happen.

In 2011 a revolution in Tunisia brought about the first free democratic elections in 55 years.

The commentators who had predicted this would happen, though 8 years earlier, optimistically labelled the movement 'the Arab Spring.'

Pro-reform protests did indeed manifest across northern Africa and the Middle East. Muammar Gadaffi was overthrown in Libya. Hosni Mubarak was ousted in Egypt.

In other nations the insurgency was minor or met with fierce government resistance.

Of the three nations where regime change occurred only Tunisia seems to have a relatively stable government. Egypt quickly reverted to authoritarian rule and Libya is torn by civil war.

In Syria the Arab Socialist Ba'ath Party ruled, as it had since 1961. Bashar al-Assad, the successor of his father Hafez, had been President of Syria since 2000.

His election was greeted with optimism by elements in the country eager for reform.

But Assad was not interested in political and social reform.

When the Arab Spring came to the gates of Damascus, the capital of Syria, in May 2011, it found the regime in no mood for change.

The initially peaceful protests were repressed.

In July Army defectors formed the Free Syrian Army and began recruiting.

Thus the Syrian Civil War began. As of March 2017 the government controls the capital, the principle towns in the west, and the coast

The anti-government factions control, in general, the north and south-east of the country.

Added into the mix is of course ISIS., which controls the west.

Enter Vladimir Putin.

Putin has mocked, and perhaps justifiably, the US idea of forcing democracy on regimes or 'the export of revolutions', as he termed it.

During a face to face meeting in September 2015, he told President Obama 'instead of the triumph of democracy and progress, we got violence, poverty and social division.'

The United States Middle Eastern policy had been a disaster. The 2003 invasion of Iraq, initiated by Obama's predecessor George W Bush, had caused a monumental shift in power. US troops and allied forces were involved in the subsequent Iraq insurgency and civil war until 2011.

Still Obama was determined to effect regime change. He urged Putin to support him. Assad would step down and allow free elections.

Putin refused. Syria was an old ally of Russia. During the Cold War the Soviet Union provided help in the formation of the Syrian Arab Army.

In 1955 the Baghdad Pact created an alliance of four Middle Eastern countries – Turkey, Iran, Iraq and Pakistan, plus the United Kingdom. It was engineered by the United States ostensibly against the Soviet Union.

Syria however perceived that it was aimed at itself as well and drew closer to Moscow.

In 1966 the Soviet Union supported the coup that brought Assad's father to power. Moscow was rewarded in 1971 when Syria leased the naval facility in the port of Tartus to the Soviet Union.

Tartus is Russia's only Mediterranean naval base and so is vital to Russia's interests.

Also important to Russia is a pipeline under construction that would transport natural gas from Iraq through Syria for export to Europe.

Now Russia has the largest reserves of natural gas in the world. Iran has the second largest. Iran is a friend of Russia. So if Russia has power over the Iranian pipeline it would control most of Europe's energy supply.

This would be something the European Union and the United States could not permit.

This helps to explain why the United States and the EU are determined to get Assad out, and why the Russian Federation backs him.

However Putin's support for Assad may also be seen in the context of Putin's broader foreign policy – keeping the United States and the European Union away from Russia's borders and reasserting the sphere of influence it exercised during the Soviet era.

Putin's first direct intervention in the civil war began in September 2015. Assad requested Russian military assistance. The rebels were being supplied with US funds and weapons, though Obama had emphatically ruled out sending US troops.

On the 30th Russian planes began a series of raids against the Free Syrian Army as well as ISIS positions.

Obama protested, but again, would not commit ground troops to help the Syrian rebels. He could not risk a clash with Russian forces and besides, the American public had no appetite for another long and probably unwinnable war, such as Iraq had been.

While this book is being written the situation is dramatically changing.

In 2016 Donald Trump became President of the United States. Elected on a platform of isolationism, he appeared to have a hands-off approach toward Syria.

This suited Putin perfectly. Later on we will look at the probability that Putin helped put Trump in the Whitehouse.

On April 4 2017 warplanes attacked the rebel-held town of Khan Sheikhoun in north-western Syria.

They dropped chemical bombs.

At the time of writing 86 civilians are reported dead with many more injured. The death toll is likely to rise. There were no military casualties.

The United States affirmed that government planes dropped the gas bombs. The Syrian and Russian governments denied this.

This was not the first time outlawed chemical weapons had been used in the Syrian Civil War. There have been at least 64 other reported uses of chemical weapons.

Targets have been mostly rebel - held areas, though rebel forces have also used them.

Barack Obama had told Assad that the use of chemical weapons was a 'red line. Yet when the Syrian government did employ those weapons Obama did nothing to risk a confrontation with Putin.

Then on April 7 US ships fired 59 Tomahawk missiles on the Syrian government airbase at Homs. US intelligence had determined that the planes which launched the chemical attacks came from this base.

The attack stunned the world, drawing praise from many, and condemnation from others. It was made without the knowledge of the United States Congress or the United Nations.

Trump had consistently stated that he would not involve the US military in the Syrian Civil War.

Putin condemned the strike, calling it an illegal act of aggression and a violation of international law. He warned of 'extremely serious' consequences.

Putin suspended an agreement with the US on the prevention of air incidents, meaning that the risk of Russian and US planes accidentally clashing has increased.

Furthermore Putin ordered a frigate to the eastern Mediterranean.

Iran, Syria's close ally, also condemned the strike.

Putin's Other Hotspots

Putin's foreign policy shares the same characteristics as that of the United States, China or the European Union. He wishes to create a sphere of influence that will buffer his nation against incursions from other powers.

To this end Russia wishes to dominate the former states of the Soviet Union and resist the influence of the United States in the Middle East.

The United States has a policy of dominating all the oceans of the world so to prevent an attack upon the United States. This is not so different to Putin's policy of dominating all the land routes to Russia.

The US maritime sphere of influence includes the Mediterranean Sea, the Baltic Sea - both vital to Russia's interests as well - as well as the South China Sea where China also has interests.

There have been other hotspots on the earthquake zone where both Russian and US have clashed.

One of these is the Republic of Georgia, which lies in the Caucasus Mountains. Its southern border touches Turkey, Armenia and Azerbaijan. The Russian Federation faces Georgia in the north.

Georgia was part of the Soviet Union until it dissolved in 1991.

Georgia, like many states of the former Soviet empire, is ethnically diverse, though Georgians predominate.

Not long after Georgia declared independence it expressed a wish for ties with the United States and the European Union.

Georgia began receiving economic and military aid from the United States and initiated talks with a view to joining NATO and the EU.

This worried the Russian Federation, which with justification feared it was being surrounded by the West.

The Baltic States – Lithuania, Latvia and Estonia – had come within the US sphere of influence. So too had the former satellite states of the Soviet Union: Poland, Hungary, Romania, Bulgaria and the Czech Republic.

The former Yugoslavia was breaking up and the US/EU alliance was bringing the successor states on side.

The Caspian to Mediterranean oil pipeline was also of interest to Putin.

This line ran from Baku in Azerbaijan through to Tblisi, the capital of Georgia, and ended at Ceyhan in Turkey.

The pipeline company was established in 2002. The project was completed in 2005.

Globally the pipeline is not significant in itself, supplying as it does only 1 % of the world's oil.

Regionally however it is of great significance. It enriches Russia's southern neighbors and increases US influence in the region. Putin fears that the US could send troops to the Caucasus to defend the pipeline.

Georgia and Russia came to blows over the Ossetian and Abkhaz regions within Georgia.

When Georgia became independent in 1991 the Abkhaz in the west and the Ossetians in the east demanded independence.

Georgia went to war with the province of South Ossetia (North Ossetia being still under Russian rule). The South Ossetians were supported by Russia. In 1992 a ceasefire was brokered which left the question of South Ossetian independence unresolved.

Abkhazia also revolted, again with Russian support, with again, no resolution being reached.

In the year 2000 Putin was Prime Minister of the Russian Federation, and relations with Georgia further declined.

In August 2008 South Ossetian rebels began shelling Georgian villages. In response the Georgian Army moved into South Ossetia, where Russian peace-keeping forces were stationed.

Putin and President Medvedev accused Georgia of unwarranted aggression and ordered an invasion of Georgia on August 8. Abkhaz forces joined the attack.

Russian planes bombed the Georgian capital and attempted to destroy the Baku pipeline.

With the Russian and Ossetian forces less than 60 km away from Tbilisi, the Georgians agreed to a ceasefire negotiated by French President Nicolas Sarkozy.

Russian forces withdrew from Georgia, but Russia nevertheless officially recognized the republics of South Ossetia and Abkhazia.

This was greeted with widespread international condemnation. Georgia cut off all diplomatic ties with the Russian Federation.

Russia continues to maintain military bases in South Ossetia and Abkhazia.

As far as Putin is concerned the Georgian war achieved its aims. It eliminated the prospects of Georgia entering the NATO alliance and has undermined US hegemony.

Putin continues to exercise influence over the two regions. In March 2017 the South Ossetian armed forces were incorporated into the Russian army.

Staying in the Caucasus region we now look at Chechnya.

Chechnya is located on the Georgian border and also shares a border with South Ossetia. There are over a 1 million people there and the chief city is Grozny. Most of the people are Muslims.

When the Soviet Union dissolved the Chechens wished to declare independence.

Boris Yeltsin did not permit this, arguing that Chechnya had never been an autonomous nation within the Soviet Union as Ukraine, Lithuania, Estonia, Latvia and other Soviet republics had been.

Russian forces and Chechens fought in the First Chechen War from 1990 to 1996.

The conflict proved difficult for the Russians, the Chechens having the advantage of mountains for defense. In an assault on Grozny lasting three months the Russians lost 1997 tanks, more than had been lost during the 1945 Battle of Berlin.

The progress of the war was politically damaging to President Yeltsin, and probably contributed to his decision to hand over power to Putin.

A ceasefire was eventually signed. Russians troops withdrew and the Chechens elected a government.

The President of Chechnya, Aslan Maskadov, steered an unsteady course between asserting Chechen independence and asking Russia for help in rebuilding his devastated country.

Russia was happy to do this. Along with aid the Russian government sent two brigades of troops.

Most of the funds were distributed amongst local Chechen warlords. Corruption was rife. The warlords made money out of kidnapping. In fact the proceeds of kidnapping became the primary source of the country's income.

Maskadov's attempts to reign in the corruption led to an outbreak of political and religious violence.

In August 1999 a group of armed religionists calling themselves the Islamic International Brigade crossed into neighboring Dagestan, hoping to free it from Russian rule.

The invasion failed. Putin, now President of Russia, had learnt the lessons of the First Chechen War and invaded Chechen with a well-planned strategy.

Grozny fell in February 2000.

Insurgency in the Muslim Caucasus continues to this day. The jihadist Emirate of the Caucasus wishes to establish an independent Islamic state. Likewise Islamic State (ISIS) is active in the region.

Putin resists the influence of western forces from outside Russia. He also resists it within Russia.

The Russian Constitution recognizes 'fundamental' and 'inalienable' human rights. Some of these rights are not specifically mentioned in comparable constitutions, including the right to one's good name and honor, privacy, freedom of communication and freedom of travel.

Freedom of religion, the press, liberty to express one's views, the right of free association and participation in society are all acknowledged and protected under the Constitution.

The Constitution even goes so far as to oblige all citizens to 'preserve nature and the environment.'

Russia is a signatory to the European Convention on Human Rights.

Nevertheless the European Court on Human Rights regularly accepts cases from Russia.

On June 1 2007 22% of the Court's caseload involved Russian litigants. These cases cover deaths in custody, torture, rape, murder of ethnic minorities, kidnapping, execution without trial and cruelty against children.

Much institutional cruelty, abuse and corruption carried over from the Soviet regime. However there seems to be little effort to seriously end these/

Indeed the limitations on liberty and abuses of power perpetrated by the Communist regime seem to be returning under Putin.

As part of a swathe of measures ostensibly targeting terrorism, Putin enacted a law in 2012 which allows non-government organizations within Russia to be regarded as 'foreign agents'.

NGOs are required to register with the state. In 2015 a further law allows the state to shut down any of these 'foreign agents' deemed to be a threat to national security.

So far seven of these have been banned. All are US-based pro-democracy institutions.

Freedom of Assembly, though protected unconditionally by the Constitution, is severely restricted. At first these restrictions amounted to giving authorities notice of demonstrations.

Since 2014 however demonstrations must be authorized. Even individuals picketing alone may be fined or imprisoned for up to 5 years.

Human Rights Watch reported that the first person to be imprisoned (for 2 and a half years) under this legislation was Ildar Dadin. In 2016 Dadin alleged that he was beaten and degraded in the prison colony of Segheza in northern Russia.

In December 2015 Putin signed a law that gave the Constitutional Court of Russia the right to determine whether the rulings of international legal bodies, such as the European Court of Human Rights can be deemed to contradict the Russian Constitution and hence have no legal effect.

The Chairman of the Constitutional Court is nominated by the President.

Media outlets and publishers are now obliged to declare foreign funding.

Law enforcement agencies are empowered by law to place on watch lists persons or organizations deemed to be engaging in 'anti-social behavior' or in actions 'contrary to commonly accepted norms of behavior and morality.'

Putin has cracked down on the Internet. The Duma has passed legislation requiring search engine owners with more than 1 million users to be accountable for the content on their sites.

Further, Russian language search engines must be owned by Russians, opening the way for state supervision of online companies.

Freedom of religion, guaranteed by the Constitution, is also under threat. We have already touched upon the law forbidding religious activity outside places of worship.

But restrictions had existed even before Putin came to power.

President Yeltsin signed the Law on Freedom of Conscience and Religious Associations in 1997, after having unsuccessfully vetoed the bill.

The law defines a religious organization as an institution possessing a creed, regular worship services and religious education.

This definition would exclude institutions such as the Salvation Army and Evangelical Christian groups which do not have defined services and places of worship.

According to the law, religious organizations must be registered with the state. Moreover, they cannot engage in public activity until 15 years after registration.

This provision favors 'traditional' Russian religions: Orthodoxy, Catholicism, Islam, Judaism and Buddhism. New religions are restricted.

In practice the Russian Orthodox Church was exempt from these restrictions.

The law came into effect through the co-operation of the Russian Orthodox Church, secular nationalists and Communists, all of whom had an interest in restricting the free exercise of religion.

Religions targeted by the 1997 law include the Church of Scientology, Jehovah's Witnesses and the Unification Church.

Relations between the Catholic Church and Russian Orthodox Church have always been tense.

There are over 5 million Catholics in Russia. Over 4 million of these belong to the Ukrainian Greek Catholic Rite, which separated from the Russian Orthodox Church and placed themselves under the Pope in 1596.

Catholicism is viewed with disfavor by the Russian state (and historically, other authoritarian governments) because its head is outside the country.

For this reason the Catholic Church in Russia was oppressed by the Tsars and especially persecuted under the Soviet Union.

Under Yeltsin and Putin the old Russian fears of foreign influence through Catholicism remains.

Pope John Paul II (1978 – 2004), wishing to mend relations with the Russian Orthodox Church, greatly desired to visit Russia, but the Russian Church resisted his overtures.

One of the most antipathetic voices belonged to Vsevolod Chaplin, whom we have seen in a previous chapter as Putin's personal chaplain and spiritual advisor.

In 2002 the Vatican appointed the Polish Jerzy Mazur Bishop of St Joseph at Urkutsk. The diocese to which he was appointed is in eastern Siberia, and has been described as the largest Catholic diocese in the world.

Mazur was refused entry at Moscow airport. Mazur had lived in Russia before and had applied for Russian citizenship.

The ban followed an accusation by the Russian Church that the Roman Church was attempting to win converts in Russia.

Patriarch Aleksi called the Catholic influence an 'invasion'. Putin called the Vatican's choice of bishops 'tactless.'

Archbishop Tadeusz Kondrusiewicz, Catholic Archbishop of Minsk complained of 'an organized campaign against Russia's Catholic Church.'

Since Mazur other Catholic priests have been denied visas.

Homosexual, bisexual and transgendered person have also been the target of restrictive laws,

Though sex between consenting same-sex adults was decriminalized in 1993 there are no protections against discrimination.

There has been increased discrimination as well as acts of violence against homosexuals, particularly in the larger cities such as St

Petersburg and Moscow where gay communities have thrived.

Under the Soviet Union homosexuality was first decriminalized by Lenin. However Stalin again made same-same relationships illegal and punishable by hard labor. However the law only affected men. Thousands were sentenced during the Soviet period.

The constitutional laws guaranteeing personal freedoms officially remain. President Putin has committed himself to them. Nevertheless he turns a blind eye to regional governments discriminating against homosexual and transgendered persons.

Requests for a Gay Pride march in Moscow have been repeatedly denied. An attempt to hold one in 2009 was broken up, with all 30 participants arrested.

In March 2012 the Russian Ministry of Justice made the state's attitude in the matter explicit when it refused permission for a Pride House – a safe place for homosexual and transgendered athletes to gather – to be established during the 2014 Winter Olympics held in Sochi.

Pride Houses had begun in 2010.

The Ministry of Justice stated that the organization of a Pride House would incite 'propaganda of non-traditional sexual orientation which can undermine the security of the Russian society and the state, provoke social-religious hatred, which is the feature of the extremist character of the activity.'

In June 2013 Putin and the State Duma enacted a law prohibiting the dissemination of 'propaganda of non-traditional sexual relationships' to minors.

Putin defended the law as a protection of 'traditional Russian values.'

The law was promoted by the Russian Orthodox Church and other conservatives groups.

It was passed in the Duma without opposition. One parliamentarian abstained.

Many Russians interpreted the law as giving them license to perpetrate harassment and violence against gay, lesbian and transgendered people.

In May 2013, not long after the passage of the law, a 23 year old man was beaten and killed in Volgograd, simply for admitting his sexual orientation to his friends.

Vigilante groups started humiliating and bashing targeted individuals.

Human Rights Watch reports that violence is widespread across Russia, and that enforcement agencies rarely do anything to stop or prevent the violence.

Requests for protection and prosecution are habitually ignored. There is no law prohibiting the harassment of individuals on account of their sexuality.

Putin himself ignores the violence.

Many gay, lesbian, bisexual and transgendered people are fleeing their country or seeking asylum from countries like the United States.

Putin is obsessed with what he calls 'traditional Russia,' the 'Holy Russia' of Tsarist times - the kingdom of heaven on earth.

Taking his inspiration from Orthodox Christianity he seems to believe that Russia has a sacred mission. In order that Russia should fulfil its destiny she needs to be purified, purged of barbaric foreign influences and ideas.

He is apparently quite sincere when he labels homosexuality a threat to Russian security.

He is sure that Orthodoxy is the only authentic expression of Russian spirituality and those others are a threat to it.

For him the United States and western liberalism is the foreigner and the barbarian at the gates which Ilyin and Solovyov warned of.

That is why Putin believes there had to be war in Georgia, why Assad must stay in

Syria and why Ukraine should be dismembered.

Putin once made this statement about being a conservative leader: 'the point of conservatism is not that it prevents movement forward and upward, but that it prevents movement backward and downward, into chaotic darkness and a return to a primitive state.'

Putin believes he is holding back the forces of chaos.

For Putin there are two great conflicting forces governing the world. The first is Orthodox Russian civilization. The second is liberal democracy professing freedom, but without a clear vision of where it wants to go; in other words, chaos.

Putin and Trump

On November 8 2016 the businessman and television personality Donald Trump was famously and spectacularly elected to the highest office in the United States.

During his campaign and after his election the nature of his relationship with President Vladimir Putin has been the subject of much scrutiny. The issue has dogged him and continues to do so.

During the election campaign Trump praised Putin as a strong leader even as the FBI, CIA and other agencies were alerting President Obama to the discovery that Russia had hacked the computers of Hilary Clinton's Democratic campaign.

Trump dismissed these claims as 'ridiculous'. As President – Elect he refuted the intelligence agencies without offering any proof.

Then Obama's administration expelled 35 Russian diplomats in retaliation for the hacks.

Russia responded by saying it would wait until Trump assumed office before taking action.

Trump bewildered many by saying Putin had been 'very smart' not to immediately respond to these expulsions. This led to questions about what exactly Trump knew about the situation and why Putin would wait until Trump took office.

Donald Trump has done business with Russia. He has travelled to Russia several times for talks with developers and government officials to discuss projects.

His son Donald Trump Jnr declared in 2008 that a 'disproportionate' amount of Trump's assets came from Russia, and that 'a lot of money' came from Russia.

Some of Trump's real estate deals outside of Russia have been financed by Russian oligarchs.

Trumps dealings with Russia go back long before the Putin era. In 1986 he wanted to build hotels in Russia. The project never came to fruition. Nevertheless he saw Russia as a fresh market ready to be exploited.

Due to restrictive government regulations Trump never made the impact in Russia that he desired. However he established strong ties with Russian investors.

In 2013 he brought the Miss Universe Pageant to Moscow, in partnership with the Russian billionaire oligarch Aras Agalarov.

At the time he tweeted 'do you think Putin will be going to The Miss Universe Pageant in November in Moscow - if so, will he become my new best friend?'

Trump hoped that Agalarov would give him access to Putin.

Putin did not attend the Miss Universe Pageant. But Trump was invited to call upon

Herman Gref, head of the state-controlled Sberbank PJSC, the largest bank in the Russian Federation.

Trump's visit suggests that Trump is close to officials in the Kremlin, if not to Putin himself.

President Putin himself has said that he is 'not acquainted with Trump.' Trump on the other hand has claimed to have met the Russian leader on at least two occasions.

During a 2013 interview Trump claimed to have a 'relationship' with Putin.

However on January 11 2017 he vehemently distanced himself from the Russian leader.

'Russia has never tried to leverage me,' the President-Elect tweeted days before taking office. 'I HAVE NOTHING TO DO WITH RUSSIA - NO DEALS. NO LOANS. NO NOTHING.'

On one level a meeting of minds between Putin and Trump seems unlikely. Trump epitomizes everything Putin despises about the West.

Trump's flamboyant, brash style, his arrogance and confidence in the power and righteousness of unfettered capitalism – these would seem to clash with Putin's sombre, conservative, highly regulated and disciplined Russia.

On the other hand the two men share certain characteristics. Both are extremely wealthy. Both understand power. Both live in opulence and exercise a personal mystique, though Trump seems to possess a more narcissistic personality.

According to Mikhail Fishman, editor of the Moscow Times, a paper critical of Putin, the Kremlin sees Trump as something of a buffoon.

Moscow saw President Trump as a 'useful idiot' who could be manipulated by Putin to Russia's advantage.

Putin is clearly more experienced than Trump, and he saw his narcissism and admiration for himself as a weakness to be exploited.

Links between Russia and the Trump presidential campaign have been revealed.

A number of members of the campaign team, including Chairman Paul Manafort met Russian intelligence officials repeatedly during 2016.

Lieutenant General Michael Flynn, appointed National Security Advisor to President Trump, at first denied having communications with Russia. Later he confirmed that he had contacts with the Russian Ambassador Sergey Kislyak, and has since resigned.

The new Attorney General, Jeff Sessions, likewise denied meeting the Ambassador twice. After being forced to confirm that he had he recused himself from the investigation into Russian interference in the 2016 election.

It was also revealed that Donald Trump's son-in-law Jared Kushner, appointed a senior advisor to his father-in-law, also had contacts with the Russian Ambassador as well as other officials.

Other revelations followed. Carter Page, a former foreign policy to Trump, admitted to meeting Kislyak.

Erik Prince, a major contributor to the Trump campaign and founder of a private military company, with a Russian official close to Putin, with the aim of establishing a line of communication between the Trump team and the Kremlin.

The so- called Steele Dossier was also of considerable concern.

In January both President Obama and President - Elect Trump were presented with documents produced by an intelligence agent identified as Christopher Steele.

The contents of the dossier claim to reveal that the Kremlin had compromising information about Donald Trump that could be used to blackmail him, and that the Russians had in fact worked to have him elected.

The dossier was considered credible enough to be brought to the attention of the President and President- Elect. But Trump responded with a blistering attack on the intelligence services for attaching any value to it.

He similarly attacked the media outlet Buzzfeed for publishing the contents of the dossier, calling it 'fake news.'

Amongst the most lurid of the allegations in the dossier is the suggestion that Trump engaged in 'perverted sexual acts' in a Russian hotel.

Putin was looking forward to a Trump presidency. Trump professed to be an isolationist, as the presidents of the United

States had been before World War II. He would put 'America first.'

To Putin this would mean hands – off approach toward Russia. During his campaign Trump had criticized the European Union and NATO. He rounded on US allies for taking advantage of the United States.

He praised Putin in Syria for attacking ISIS, though the weakening of the Syrian rebels - not ISIS, was Putin's first objective.

In the US Congress and in the media around the world the question was being asked - how much did Trump himself know about the contacts between his campaign team and the Kremlin in 2016/17?

Was there collusion between the two to damage the Clinton campaign and win the presidency for Trump? If so, was Trump himself privy to the conspiracy?

If Trump was complicit he was liable to be impeached.

Then on March 4 Trump suddenly and dramatically claimed that President Obama had bugged Trump Tower, his New York Headquarters, during the election campaign.

'How low has President Obama gone to tap (sic) my phones during the very sacred election process,' he tweeted. 'This is Nixon/Watergate. Bad (or sick) guy!'

Former Whitehouse officials denied this ever happened, and Trump himself refused to offer any justification or explanation of his claims.

Trump's explosive accusation occurred at the same time that Jeff Sessions was being asked to explain his formerly denied contact with the Russian Ambassador.

Trump asked Congress to investigate his claim.

Meanwhile the congressional investigation into links between Trump and Russia was headed by Republican Devin Nunes.

Nunes had served on the Trump team during the transition to the Whitehouse. He had denied that there was evidence linking the Trump team to Russian agents and had said that he would not investigate the now disgraced Michael Flynn's ties with them.

Nunes learnt that federal intelligence agencies had indeed collected information about the Trump campaign. However neither Trump nor any member of his team had been targeted.

Instead the information had been collected incidentally. The targets were actually foreign agents, presumably Russian. The investigation was perfectly legal.

Nunes went to the Whitehouse directly and told this to Trump, before sharing this information with the rest of the investigating committee.

He was widely criticized for this action, and called upon to recuse himself from the investigation into the Trump-Russia connection.

Then Trump, in typical fashion, acted suddenly and completely unexpectedly.

We have seen how Syrian civilians were bombed with nerve gas at Khan Shaykun on April 4 2017.

On April 7 Trump ordered an attack on Shayrat Air Base, from where the bombers allegedly came.

Trump himself said the attack was in retaliation for the bombings and to deter Syria from using chemical weapons again.

A number of commentators have suggested that the real motive was domestic in nature.

They believe that Trump wanted to distance himself from Putin and demonstrate that he was not beholden to him.

If that was the case, Trump was prepared to take the world to the edge of war for the sake of his political security.

As we have seen, Putin reacted severely to Trump's strike, calling it illegal and an act of aggression.

Putin's spokesman declared that US- Russian relations had been 'substantially impaired'.

The Russian Prime Minister, Dmitri Medvedev, stated that the United States 'was on the verge of a military clash with Russia.'

The allies of the United States, including those at enmity with Russia, such as Ukraine, Georgia, Latvia, Lithuania and Turkey, supported the US strike and expressed their solidarity with President Trump.

Reversing his own policy, Trump now declared that there could be no peace in Syria with Assad in power. He had previously blasted Obama for his policy of regime change in Syria.

Also contradicting his election campaign, he declared support for the NATO alliance. In a news conference several days after the strike he linked the strength and importance of NATO to the overthrow of the Assad regime.

This was surely as red rag to a bull for Putin.

The missile bearing warship Admiral Grigorovich was dispatched by the Russian President to the eastern Mediterranean shortly after the strike.

As this book is written the US Secretary of State, Rex Tillerson, goes to Russia to demand that Putin reign in Assad.

There is little likelihood that the President will do so.

At the same time a US flotilla heads toward North Korea, following an ultimatum from the United States to the end that that country stops its nuclear program.

North Korean leader Kim Jon-Un has threatened to launch a nuclear attack against the United States if provoked.

150 000 Chinese troops are mobilizing on the North Korean border.

The writer sincerely hopes that when you read this the world is still at peace.

The Third World War

If war did break out between Russia and the United States and their respective allies, what would it look like?

In terms of troops, tanks, ships, weapons, etc., the United States is clearly more powerful than the Russian Federation.

According to MilitaryTimes the United States can field 1,350 000 soldiers. Russia has 845 000.

The US has over 1,400 m military planes. Russia has 1,200.

Russia has 218 warships, including only 1 aircraft carrier. The US has 282, including 10 aircraft carriers.

US submarines: 71. Russian: 59.

The US spends 560 billion a year on its military. Russia spends $60 billion.

On top of US firepower we can consider the forces of NATO and the non –NATO US allies such as Japan, the Philippines, Mexico, South Korea, Israel and Australia.

The one advantage Russia could be said to have in terms of its arsenal is its nuclear weapons. They have 7,700 to America's 7,100.

It has been observed that the gap between the Russian and US military is narrowing quickly.

In a way the superiority of the US Navy doesn't matter to Russia. Russia is a land – based power. The US is anxious to control the seas because it is surrounded by ocean.

Russia does not need to control the oceans but it does need access to the Black and Baltic Seas.

Russia would be reluctant to face US forces directly.

But it wouldn't necessarily have to. Russia is such a vast country that invading it would be almost impossible. In the past Napoleon and Hitler both realized the logistical nightmare of war in Russia.

Russia would probably knock out its smaller western neighbors fairly easily. The Baltic states of Latvia, Lithuania and Estonia would be reincorporated into the Russian empire. Ukraine is on the verge of breakdown anyway. The tiny republics in the Caucasus could not resist a Russian incursion.

As allies Russia would have Syria and Iran. Belarus has economic and political links with the Russian Federation and would probably side with Russia.

It is unknown where China would stand in the event of a war between Russia and the

West. Putin has done much to mend the relationship, damaged during the Soviet era.

China is not really interested in other nation's wars. However it is interested in protecting its seas against American aggression. If Putin and America came to blows in the Pacific China might well intervene.

In any case Russia could at least rely on China's neutrality.

With Iran protecting Russia's Middle Eastern interests and the central Asian republics (Kazakhstan, Uzbekistan and Turkmenistan) acting as buffers, and with Iraq too fractured to safely host US bases, it is likely that Russia would only have to fight on its western border.

Throw into this the Islamic extremist factor which would be inflamed by an increased US presence in the Middle East. Terrorist attacks by ISIS and other groups would increase in US – aligned countries.

The chief battlegrounds would be Border countries where NATO has bases: Latvia, Lithuania, Estonia, and Poland.

Turkey is also a member of NATO and the fight for the control of the Black Sea would be a fierce one.

Ukraine of course would be a front line and Putin would be anxious to crush its military because NATO troops could establish a foothold there.

Russia would be unlikely to defeat NATO forces outright but then again, NATO would be unlikely to be able to conquer Russia.

Then there are the nuclear weapons. If pushed to the brink, might one side or another dare to launch a missile? No-one could possibly win a nuclear war and both sides of the conflict would know it.

Nevertheless the world has come to the brink of nuclear war at least 11 times since the only nuclear bombs used in war were dropped on Hiroshima and Nagasaki in 1945.

The last scare was on October 23 2010 50 Intercontinental Ballistic Missiles (IBMs) went offline for 45 minutes and were beyond control. It was feared the hackers were attempting to take over the system and launch the missiles.

Cyberwarfare is a new element in military technology. Hostile experts could hijack missiles and other weapons systems.

One might surmise that if Putin could hack into the US Presidential Election he could hack the US Military.

Vladimir Putin's term of office ends in 2018. He may stand for election a second time, in which case he would be President of Russia until 2024.

There seems little doubt that he would be elected. The United Russia Party shows no signs of disillusionment with him.

Perhaps he will anoint a successor. Right now he doesn't seem to be mentoring anyone for the succession.

Perhaps he will change the Constitution and allow himself to be elected for life.

Or it may be that Putin is crowned Tsar of Russia in name as well as fact, and he will be the founder of a dynasty.

It may be that the fate of Putin, and of all Russia, depends on how he handles the present confrontation with the West.

Whatever happens to Vladimir Putin in his own future, he holds our futures in his hands now.

Printed in Great Britain
by Amazon